Story Index

The cluster of stories are, Page 4: Cornwall; Page 6: St Just-in-Roseland; Page 8: Lanhydrock; Page 10: Tintagel Island; Page 12: Cotehele; Page 14: Porthcurno; Page 16: St Michael's Mount; Page 20: Gunwalloe; Page 22: Carn Brea; Page 24: Lelant; Page 26: Cape Cornwall; Page 28: Roche Rock; Page 30: Daymer Bay; Page 32: Cardinham; Page 34: Purpose of Living.

Picture Index

Front Cover: Botallack; Inside Front Cover/1: Tresillian River; Page 3: Temple Church; Page 5: Hemmick Beach; Page 7: St Just-in-Roseland; Page 9: Lanhydrock; Page 11: Tintagel; Page 13: Cotehele; Page 15: Minack Theatre, Porthcurno; Page 17: St Michael's Mount; Page 18/19: Botallack; Page 21: Gunwalloe; Page 23: Carn Brea; Page 25: Porth Kidney Sands from Lelant Dunes; Page 27: Cape Cornwall; Page 29: Rock Roche; Page 31: Daymer Bay; Page 33: Cardinham; Page 35: Alex Tor, Bodmin Moor; Inside Back Cover: Harlyn Bay; Back Cover: St Just-in-Roseland.

Introduction

A Sanctuary is defined as a refuge, a shelter, a holy place. On Bodmin Moor, during the 12th Century, in the sacred hamlet of Temple, the Order of The Knights Templar established a peaceful place, for the travellers to rest in total protection, before returning to an arduous journey full of serious danger.

Today, there is a tendency to be swept along in the modern world of rush and hum drum, of chasing irrelevant goals. The old ways of nature have become lost in the mists of time, but amidst the besiege of money searching gains and endless material needs, should be found the time to visit ageless sanctuaries, where you can overwhelm yourself with amazing feelings, which enrich your soul, and make you realise the purpose of life is very different to the existing method of living.

This book is dedicated to those places that calm the soul, inspire the spirit and open the eyes to the glory of living. Let us venture, to discover.

Cornwall

This sacred domain has a deep-rooted feeling of love, magic and mystery, that simmers quietly below the surface. There are many sanctuaries, you can discover, which elude the frantic pace of the modern world, who relentlessly attempts to erode the old ways.

On venturing along a quiet country lane or a leafy path, that harmonies with colourful wild flowers and the melody of hidden feathery songsters, leading to green lush valleys, filled with sweet smelling trees and busy crystal clear water cascading its way to the wild foaming sea.

This air of love, lends itself to exploration, not by the mechanical fuming beast of the 20th century, but by the pleasing and exhilarating way of rambling. The walkers delve serendipitously into this pulsating loving land of legend and superstition, and sometimes on visiting a crumbling ruin or even a seemingly ordinary Church, there is something else, a feeling of peace and contentment, that can surprise the visitors.

The area becomes hazy, by the fact that you are drawn in, until you become part of it, which transports you back to a time in the distant past, when the way of nature was held totally sacred, and the vibranting spirit of the earth intermingled with the vision of the people.

This feeling, alters your perception of life. Standing quietly in a secluded, tranquil woodland in Cornwall, the sun glows with golden rays, the summer breeze filters through leaf enriched trees, the water journeys from the clouds, to streams, to rivers, to oceans, before being evaporated and ascending back to the clouds.

A deer rushes by, on route to another place, in another world. A hare hops by, searching food for his hungry family. A blackbird sings song of exquisite beauty high on a swaying branch. The bluebells infiltrate the green grass covered ground, butterflies and dragonflies add to the moving colourful environment, buzzing bees move from one beautiful flower to another. In these serene locations, life is forever progressing onwards.

For the rest of the day, through probing these peaceful atmospheric wonders, and enriching our bodies with incredible perceptions, we can use these immense feelings to fortify our lives for ever.

So now, let us continue to explore more sanctuaries with timeless tranquillity in Sacred Cornwall.

St Just-in-Roseland

A Legend is important. It gives meaning to life. It is difficult to formulate, difficult to prove and sometimes difficult to ignore. It continues to bubble beneath the surface of life, and ends up as being essential to the way of living.

Cornwall has an abundance of legends and places of paradise, and accordingly, St Just-in-Roseland's church is pure heaven. It is beautifully situated, and described by many as the most picturesque churchyard in England. It enhances the expression Sacred Cornwall and a legend is born, that satisfies the very needs of our soul, and gives comfort and fortitude to our spirit.

Remoteness is another element of this area. Travelling along minor roads and river crossings are the only routes to journey, treading this green and pleasant land. From Truro, it is possible to venture over the river on the King Harry Ferry, which is one of Cornwall's oldest crossing places. In the past it transported troops of King Charles and Oliver Cromwell. The placid and gentle trips through magical, mysterious, memorable lanes, viewing interesting properties, and places far from the modern world, leads to the eventual view of the blessed and holy Church, set in a Cornish equivalent of the Garden of Eden.

Situated in a secluded creek, the river gently washes the shore, the sun glows brightly, sending rays of warmth. Through entering the lychgate and to descend upon the churchyard, its hillside is filled with the fertility of picturesque abundance of flowers and shrubs. The air is enriched with the scented aroma, as you walk along the historic path to the Church.

You need to be here, to discover, whether the legend is fact or fiction, for this awe-inspiring domain has a mystic mood of exquisite tranquillity and eternal peace that has existed for many centuries.

2,000 years ago, Joseph of Arimathea, a tin merchant, reputedly traded in the area, would have brought his Nephew here, seems possible. However, when the relative is said to be Jesus, the Saviour of Mankind, his presence in St Just-in-Roseland is more than mere words can describe. Your soul drinks in the warmth, the marvel, the glory. In fact the thought of being in the same location, particularly in Cornwall, where Jesus existed is truly miraculous.

Which leaves us with this amazing thought, whether this was just a legend or was it history?

Lanhydrock

This is one of the finest buildings in Cornwall, which houses many interesting rooms, that needs exploring. Lanhydrock is surrounded by acres of ravishing, picturesque woodlands and nearby the River Fowey rushes by.

Having driven from nearby Bodmin or through the Glynn Valley, park the vehicle and walk into the grounds, the first sight of the Mansion is utterly stunning. It is essentially a Victorian house, but there are older segments visible.

The name is deemed to be based on St Hydroc, an Irish missionary, whilst the estate was owned until the 1530s, by the Priory of St Petroc in Bodmin, which ended because monasteries were dissolved.

Over the next period, several people retained it, until 1620, when it was bought by Sir Richard Robartes, a masterful provincial merchant, who began to construct a period four side house on every side of a central courtyard. Unfortunately, he died in 1634. His son John, finished the building, and was a prominent Parliamentarian during the Civil War.

Few alterations were made to the Mansion over the next two centuries. There were several owners, who were MPs and helped local people. In the 1780s the east wing was dismantled, and due to lack of occupants, was in a state of disrepair, disregard and almost vacant of contents.

In the mid next century, the first Baron Robartes came to live here, and gave authority to George Gilbert Scott, the Victorian architect, to update Lanhydrock. After the improvements, twenty years later, regrettably a fire destroyed all but the north wing. This tragedy caused Lady Robartes to end her life and subsequently the Lord passed away, the next year.

Their son, Thomas, despite suffering the loss of his parents, employed Richard Coad, a local architect, to re-build the house again, which basically has been upgraded to its present superb standard.

National Trust, since 1953, has improved its contents, which overall has made a very interesting place to visit. Possibly, of the many rooms, the most splendid is the Gallery, positioned in the north wing, making it one of the older part of the Mansion. Certainly, exploring the magnificent Mansion, the very impressive and beautiful gardens, the acres of secluded woodland, and viewing the flowing River Fowey, eases the pressure of this modern world.

Tintagel Island

Most of the public, even the successful, modern business people, approaching this unique supreme area for the first time, encounter a different environment. As they venture along the holy trail into this world of total amazement, can they presume, what actually happened here?

This hallowed island is a very rocky headland, a place of wild romance and stimulating aura, with breathtaking views, of powerful waves crashing repeatedly on rugged rocks and the scent of salt water carried by the prevailing wind, intermingles with the whispering of voices from a time long, long ago.

The history is very difficult to confirm, although at one time, it was an important religious centre, housing 1,000 people. The earliest site of the Castle has Celtic roots, and was developed further over the years. The actual happening, is hidden beyond the mists of time, for you can easily fantasize and drift back to the days of King Arthur and the Knights of the Round Table, who set such high standards. But is it just fact or maybe fiction?

At the end of the day, it is considered the greatest story ever. Geoffrey of Monmouth wrote of Arthur's existence in the 12th century, though during the Victorian period, Sir Walter Scott, Charles Dickens and Alfred Lord Tennyson, developed the legend. So the idea of the quest for the Holy Grail and Arthur's drawing Excalibur from the stone, set the yardstick, which was further enhanced by the love of Guinevere and Launcelot.

Merlin the Sorcerer, who assisted Arthur, King of the Round Table, fight the evil, has a Cave dedicated to him, drilled under the land, which separates the island from the mainland. The countless stories of strange events that have taken place within the cave, make it very uncanny. The sound of the wind and waves crashing upon it, is very alarming, and attacks your being.

Tintagel Island seems ageless and serene. Physically, it has been exposed to the stormy, hailing weather, yet spiritually, it imposed a feeling of unbelievable strength. For surely, it was an ancient authority centre for the inhabitants, to develop wisdom of the universal and terrestrial foundation, and to identify the original energies conserved in nature.

Today, a journey here, takes us back to the half recalled times of yesterday, and opened our minds forever.

Cotehele

Cornwall is almost an island, as the phenomenal River Tamar nearly divides the two counties. It starts in the large coarse moorland in North Cornwall as a frivolous stream and flows for mile after mile, passing many interesting and undisturbed places. After journeying under The Tamar Bridge and The Brunel Bridge, between Saltash and Plymouth, it ventures around Drake's Island before entering into the English Channel, as a wide and deep river.

At Calstock, the railway viaduct crosses on its way from Gunnislake to Plymouth. Near here is a community in a world of its own for many years.

The woodland is marvellous and slopes high to a very quixotic Tudor House, which the Edgcumbe family maintained for 591 years, until 1944 when it was passed to the National Trust.

This is definitely a way to escape for a day, journeying from Plymouth by railway. The track is on the Devon bank next to the river. The view from the railway coach is breathtaking. Stopping in Calstock Station after crossing the viaduct, leaves you with an interesting walk to Cotehele. This area is so peaceful and has an emanate surround which stems from the ancient past.

The incredible gardens are so beautiful, with an amazing amount of various plants, shrubs and trees. The historic house was built several centuries ago. Constructed with grey granite, it is very grand. The courtyard leaves you with imagination of the days of horses and carriages. The interior has a first-class collection of household furniture and designed fittings.

Walking down to the quay, which was once a busy Victorian river port, with the view to Calstock, is magnificent, with the river winding its way to the sea. The 12 arched railway viaduct is very imposing and the sight of a train crossing, make it very exciting. The timeless quay allows you to encounter the active river, the abundance of birds, the occasional sight of a jumping fish and many different boats. From here, the trail ventures near an exuberant stream, through the enchanting woods, to intriguing places and villages.

Within the Cotehele area, interesting buildings consist of a small chapel built by Richard Edgcumbe in 1486; The Mill House and the working watermill.

At the end of the day, this visit has reduced the stress in one's life, obtaining a feeling of contentment and eagerness to encounter this tranquillity again, in the future.

Porthcurno

This name stems from the timeworn Cornish Language, which likely results as 'The Bay of Rocks'. This small village, to the east of Lands End, until the arrival of roads, was very isolated and remote from the rest of the world. Back in the faraway era, was the home of Selevan, a Celtic Saint. The sea bay is an amazing place to explore, with fine white sand and views of The Logan Rock to one side and The Minack Theatre on the other.

There appears to be only one legend here, a ghostly black square rigger, which flows over the sands, amidst the bombardments of wind and rain during the lifeless time of night, and fades away in the hazy background of the valley. The village had been the major access for telegraph cables connecting Britain to the rest of the world, which is detailed in The Museum of Submarine Telegraphy, based here.

To the east of the cove is the Iron Age cliff fort of Treryn Dinas and The Logan Rock, which is a massive granite rock weighing many, many tons and dwells poised on a cliff. Because of innumerable years of erosion, this rock is delicately balanced, and can be gently vibrated with only a little effort, at the precise spot.

Back in the 1820s, the local people were totally dismayed, when Lieutenant Goldsmith, a Royal Navy commander of the cutter HMS Nimble, with some of his crew, pushed the Logan Rock down the cliffs, probably seeking to make a famous name for himself. The Cornish people, forced the Royal Navy to restore it, to its rightful place, which took almost 60 people, over 6 months, to accomplish this gigantic task.

On the west side of the cove, situated amongst the rugged cliffs is the famous Minack Theatre, open to the swirling Cornish air elements, the sun's rays dance on the rhythmic waves in the background. The audience soon become part of the magical aura that has been generated by years of live acting here.

Rowena Cade was the inspired creator of the Theatre, during a period of over 50 years, which included the incredible construction and the difficult financial support, that never resulted in the Lady receiving income, but ended in her often using her own money to keep the Theatre alive. The first performance 'The Tempest' was in the summer of 1932. Shakespeare has been the basis over the years but there is certainly a great variety of acting during the 16 to 17 weeks summer season. Rowena Cade died in 1983, almost 90 years old and with her contributing efforts have positively set the standards and established the foundation for the future.

St Michael's Mount

This ancient artistic attraction, situated in sight of Marazion, Penzance and Mousehole, has for many, many centuries, been the base of so many incredible historic and legendary items. Visually it is totally amazing, and definitely needs a visit. The tide regularly alters the scene, which make it very unique, between being accessible by walking and detachable as an island.

This holy rocky Mount was in the past, high in the middle of an ancient wood, that is now submerged under the waters according to the misty legendary tale of the lost land of Lyonesse. The remains at low tide, were witnessed by visitors in Victorian time. Now they are in a local museum, which give basis to this being authentic history, of the sudden ocean flooding, that has been maintained to the present.

The prestigious antiquity and mysterious gathering of the hallowed Mount certainly extends back to a faraway era, known at different times, as Centre of Druid Worship and Citadel of the Sun.

St Michael the Christian Archangel of Light, responsible for restraining evil spirits and escorting souls through to the after world, was seen in 495, by a group of fishermen, standing on the rocks. This led to the most important shrine of St Michael in Britain, for pilgrims to discover. Later the many wondrous healings and disclosures improve its fame even more.

St Michael's famous ley line, an invisible form of energy, which interacts with the earth, journeys from East Anglia's most Easterly point, to Bury St Edmunds, to Glastonbury crossing the River Tamar at Horsebridge, proceeding by many Churches dedicated to St Michael, before progressing its way over St Michael's Mount, and leaving Cornwall at Carn Les Boel, near Land's End.

Over the years, the Cornish castle, which proudly overlooks the area, has been a monastic settlement, a source of peace and comfort to the pilgrims. Today it is a private place but in the past was also a fortress for the armed forces. The family of St Aubyn owned the buildings since Oliver Cromwell, and upgraded the Castle and Church to a high standard. In the 1950s it was passed to the National Trust, who have superbly marketed it.

Many famous visitors have been here, including the Royal King Charles II, Queen Victoria and Prince Albert, which leaves you walking the remarkable path to the Mount, in utter simmering delight.

Gunwalloe

Progressing through Cornwall to Helston, and finishing in the Lizard Coastline, which is a distinctively enchanted Cornish area, a territory of rare birds and animals with overwhelming wild plants and shrubs, whilst the ancient past is simmering in the atmospheric background. The modern world has yet to terminate Sacred Cornwall's wondrous feelings.

Venturing to the west side, the sea has eroded many cliffs over a period of time, and converted them into secluded coves, which is an incredible sight. St Winwaloe, Parish Church of Gunwalloe, is situated in a very exposed position to the driving waves and the harsh and rough winter gales, but has managed to overcome them so far, although the gradual rock erosion has also placed the Church under constant threat of misfortune.

Built mainly in the fifteenth century, with various thirteenth and fourteenth century components, the Church emanates a presence of interweaving wonder, mounting from years of heavenly worship.

Nearby, is the site of Winnianton, which in 1086 was a Manor controlling most of South West Cornwall. The Lord was Roger De Carminowe, a medieval Christian military campaigner and a relative of King Arthur. During that time, the Church was originally a Chapel of the Manor.

Over the years, the cove has witnessed several shipwrecks and according to several tales has buried treasures probably under the many banks of sand. In 1526, a Spanish ship was wrecked, with valuable riches worth millions of pounds now, whilst in 1785, a large seagoing vessel of the same country, met the identical disaster losing tons and tons of dollars. The notorious Buccaneer, Captain Avery, is supposed to have buried countless chests of treasure here, but despite overwhelming attempts, by numerous people, to find the hidden wealth, the cove has yet to surrender to these fortune hunters.

This sacred place is a special summer time of peaceful serenity, where the glowing sun's beams dance in glimmering pleasure, on the white froth of the smooth rhythmic waves that intermingle with the golden sand, a gentle warm breeze flows through leafy trees, and sea birds gliding in the clear sky.

This contributes to a reason to need to be here and could clear your mind of all your recent adversity.

Carn Brea

After driving through Cornwall, across Goss Moor and over the hill by Indian Queens, in the distance on the horizon appears the view of Carn Brea. These words mean rocky hill. The summit is long and on a clear day, the scenery is very interesting, for on the top is a fascinating Castle and a 19th century Monument, which obviously needs you to climb up and explore.

On arriving in Redruth and Camborne, it is evident this is the most heavily inhabited location of Cornwall, engrossed with countless industrial factors, from times long ago. Carn Brea is very distant from such affairs. It is lost in the sky, waiting for the period to change, with all the patience possible.

Mythological tales has been the retreat for legendary giants and were the reason for boulders covering this hill, when Bolster, St Agnes giant battled John of Gaunt, Carn Brea's equivalent of extraordinary size, hurling rocks around the Beacon. John has many of these large stones named after him on the hill.

The high hill is luxurious in history, working back over 5,000 years to an age of pre-historic group shelters. The remains of an enormous Neolithic hill fort, which covers approximately 46 acres, upgraded during the Iron Age and certainly was a main influence to that area during those times.

The fortified building, which at present resembles an ancient Castle, has an incredible air of mystery surrounding it. During the Medieval period, a building providently existed, but was not mentioned in writing until the 1379, when a licence was issued, by the Bishop of Exeter granting services to be held in the Chapel. From then until the present, it has been built, enlarged, updated and even vandalised, however, in the 1970s, it was bought and incredibly refurbished by Leonard Williams and converted to a restaurant.

Nearby, is the Basset Monument built in 1836, a tribute to Francis Basset, Lord de Dunstanville, who was a celebrated member of the Arts.

After journeying the steep hill, and reaching the motivating crest, one encounters the mood of time gone by, which can fire wonderful hope into your heart. The gusting wind can clear the pressure of life from your mind. Viewed from the peak, there are spectacular visual sights towards both the north and south coast, including St Agnes Beacon and scenes of many disused mine buildings. So whilst the modern world is not far away, this location seems to be another place in another time.

Lelant

The breathtaking view from the parish Church of this historic village is spectacular, situated on the cliff, near the train line that runs from St Erth to St Ives and back. Straight ahead, the outlook is across the Atlantic Ocean. The nearest land is far, far away. To the right it observes the River Hayle Estuary and Hayle's sandy beach which runs to Godrevy Point and the Lighthouse Island. Near the Church is a Golf Course and a coast path to St Ives.

The Doomsday Book 1086, has no record of this Church or even the village. In fact its first written report was 1170, when religion was infiltrated by politics and raising money, and the Church was able to gain financial income for owners. Lelant's Church is named St Uny's Church, probably named after a Christian from the fifth century. Uny is totally elusive, sometimes spelt Euny, uncertain where he was born and there is little evidence of his existence but there is an stupendous feeling here, that explains inevitably incredible happenings, that took place, but are now lost forever in the mists of time.

The Church has existed from a time long, long ago, there is an array of legends bubbling here. At the end of the day, life becomes difficult to remember. Time just simply erases all memories, but how long has the Church been here? Did the existing one, replace others? For example, Anglo-Saxon Churches have been replaced by Norman buildings in many locations. Usually a Church is in the middle of a village, so Nature can change the landscape. Now the Church is surrounded and partly buried by banks of sand, which has hidden buildings and human bodies, only for them to be rediscovered by the weather and quickly hidden again.

The sand's destructive power, totally engulfed the land, including the vicarage house. The port was here but has disappeared. In 1875, when the railway line was being laid, many skeletons were discovered, perhaps from a previous churchyard or maybe from shipwrecks. There have been earthquakes, sand and sea storms, floods and gales here, which have altered the landscape of this area tremendously and damaged the Church.

 Today it is still surviving. The feeling when near is stunning. Within the Church is a world of timeless worship and peaceful serenity. It enhances your love, which further enriches your soul. A sacred place to be married. The author wed his beautiful wife, here on the 25th September 1976.

Cape Cornwall

This is Cornwall's exclusive place named Cape, which is a headland overlooking the meeting of two oceans or channels and the crashing, frothing waves, justify the existence of the undulating, vigourous currents that never halt throughout the continuous calendar year.

Situated a few miles north of Lands End, the road journeys through Cornwall takes time and after passing through Penzance, the next place St Just, which is England's most Westerly town. A few miles further and we arrive in Cape Cornwall, which is a wild and wind-swept place that conjures up all that is untamed around the Cornish coast.

From remote area, this is a place to witness phenomenal coast views. To the south is Whitesand Bay, a picturesque mile of golden sands and to the north, Kenidjack Castle, which was constructed on the headland above the old quarry at the bottom of Kenidjack Valley, essentially an Iron Age Cliff Castle. In the present time, the relics have been overgrown by nature.

A few miles away is The Longships Lighthouse and closer the treacherous offshore rocks of Brisons, which have caused the disasters of numerous shipwrecks during the many centuries of the past. Also on these rocks is a significant hatching ground for the many types of sea birds. On a crystal-clear day, it is possible to see The Wolf Rock Lighthouse and also The Scilly Isles, which are twenty two miles away, near the glowing horizon.

The visual perceptible structure of Cape Cornwall is the aged chimney on its apex, which date back to 1850 and was constructed to benefit the boilers of this site's mine. Its shafts extended for hundreds of metres under the ground as far inland to St Just, and under the sea to The Brisons. The items extracted and brought to the surface were tin and copper, which left memories of the pioneers making fortunes from the mineral extraction.

There was once a bronze aged burial site here, situated alongside the ditches and mounds of an earlier Iron Age hill fort. Around the 4th century AD, it was the site of the first Christian chapel in West Cornwall, namely, St Helen's Oratory. The site is now occupied by a ruined farm building.

This is certainly a location full of stimulating discoveries, that absolutely enrich you, and make you realise the importance of Sacred Cornwall.

Roche Rock

Driving along the road, through the china clay area, passing one of the most dramatic sights in Cornwall, is totally stunning. You need to halt and quickly venture into an ageless, ancient place, where the timeless aura of mystic energy infiltrates your pulsating essence.

Roche Rock is to the east of the village, where the granite has risen to over a hundred feet above the area's surrounding flat ground. On the crest, built into the vital rock, is a timeworn hermitage chapel loyal to St Michael, the Christian archangel. His sacred places guard the landscape.

The raging air of mystical superstition and the lingering torment of legends is very apparent. The freakish whistling and screaming of the disruptive wind delivers, for it is obvious, existence here has been very evident.

Many stories exist, which are either myth or fact, sometimes difficult to verify, because time eventually erodes everything.

Jan Tregeagle, who abused many, many people, was eventually sentenced to perform impossible tasks for always and pleaded temporary refuge here to escape the demon hounds of Hell.

Medieval Tristan and Iseult were desperately in love with each other but despite great efforts were separated by the way of life. One of their momentary escapes was thought to have been here.

Noah's Flood is believed to have brandished away the soil, leaving the granite bare and exposed, an opportunity for the evil ones. However, eventually it became holy, as Druids and Christians fortified the area with their religious beliefs. A small building was constructed on the summit, giving the visitors a total extensive view of the picturesque territory.

Ancient story tells of St Conan, a Celtic saint, who achieved reputation as the first Bishop of Cornwall, spending time here, to speak to his God.

Late in the middle ages, the stone chapel was built to withstand the persistent lashing gales. It was eventually occupied by a solitary leper, who spent his last days there, to avoid infecting others. His daughter supplied him with water, from the mysterious well, hidden in the area.

Therefore, on visiting this location, it is apparent, you can encounter the impressions, which can filter comfortably into your investigating soul.

Daymer Bay

Driving from Wadebridge to Camelford A39 and turning to St Minver B3314, which is sign posted to Trebetherick, parking adjacent to the beach, places you in an amazing world of views, feelings and emotions.

A peaceful point of countenance with wide open spaces and a magnificent scene of the sand drenched beach and the River Camel, flowing to meet the Atlantic Ocean, with towns of Wadebridge and Padstow, nearby. It is surrounded by many superb places, which make the contents very special to attract numerous people to explore, and gives more opportunties for the young ones to use their buckets and spades in the pools located in the rocks.

Following the footpath to St Enodoc Church, leads across the very challenging golf course. On sighting the church, which is in the Parish of St Minver, is a small Norman building with a solitary jagged steeple. This has been for many, many years a very remote Church. In the past it has been buried by sand for a long period. Entrance for the only religious service of the year, was for the vicar and local clerk warden. They were carefully let down into the Church. Thankfully the Church was fully revived in the 1860s, when the sand was removed and today, religious services are still being held there.

This is the final resting place of Sir John Betjeman OBE, the poet laureate, who was very happy in Cornwall, often played on the golf course, and had a holiday retreat in Trebetherick.

In the distant past, this area was rumoured as covered by a raving forest populated by wild animals. Its creditability was established in the mid nineteenth century, when a gale roared from a very different angle and cleared an area of sand. Exposed to the world were stumps, roots of trees, horns and teeth of animals. Unfortunately, as the gale subsided, the sand returned to cover these historic objects, which leaves us today with thoughts of yesterday.

The Camel Estuary is the outstanding centre of Cornwall water sport, which mostly operates from the village of Rock, and includes sailing, windsurfing, water skiing, canoeing and rowing. Boats can be hired for many sports, and also for exploring the many sights of the tidal mouth of the river and to observe the many flowing, flying, feathery wildlife. From Rock the Black Tor ferry runs to Padstow and back. Life is very fresh and exhilarating here, and certainly a way to stimulate yourself for ever.

Cardinham

Arriving here, seems to be a remote region, where the mystery, the timelessness, the beauty, are factors of this area, that are totally staggering. Yet it is only a very few miles from the two main roads A38 Liskeard to Bodmin and the A30 Launceston to Bodmin.

Lingering in the narrow, windy lanes that go up hills and down dales, encountering the stunning aura of wonder, that suggests leaving the modern world and ready to meet people of long, long ago. For then, during those fascinating periods, the location was heavily populated.

Here are interesting places to discover. The 15th century Church is beautifully situated, imposing itself over the village, and in the churchyard is a Cornish cross, which date back to the 8th century. The old Celtic camp along the moorland skyline, is on the north side of the Churchyard, whilst on a steep hill, to the south-east of the church, Cardinham Castle, built 1080, gradually eroded away, and since the 14th century, only the earthworks exist.

Cardinham Well was one of the largest and most important holy wells ever. It existed such a long time ago, even before the Saints were here. Now there is little indication of the site, except for the bubbling stream and a stone cross. The appearance of an intense, woodland valley south west of the village of Cardinham, takes you through to a lead mine laboured in the 19th century, where silver was also discovered. There are many other mines in this area, which were being worked on until the start of the 20th century.

Cardinham Woods, managed since 1922 by the Forestry Commission, is situated on a hill and picturesque valley, that has a quiet river flowing serenely through. Venturing into the forest, by walking, running or even cycling, to discover the secluded parts of the forest. This is such a different place to be. There are so many beings and objects to see, of trees, shrubs, plants, flowers, woodland animals, birds, insects and reptiles. Changes in the seasons create many different visions and feelings, that a continual visit is very endearing.

At the end of the day, there have been so many occurences here, that the quietness now caused by the reduction in population, the encountering of ancient happenings and the exploring of the exciting woodland leave you with no doubt of its incredible wonder.

Purpose of Living

Life is difficult to define, for everyone views existence from a different body. To dwell in a building, which has functioned for many years and has had many people living there in the past, can leave you unable to know what has happened. Individually we are at different stages in life and as we battle through the modern world, time is spent earning money to pay for food, clothes and shelter. Consequently, at the end of the day, it appears to be tough to understand the purpose for living.

Love is the intangible element that exist deep in the mode of life. In the tangible course of business paperwork and meetings, love seems to have no bearing, but the emotion can effect the circumstance of people very significantly. Pure love can provide one with so much purpose for living. It can overcome all problems and turn them into opportunities.

There are times when I am asleep, I dream of travelling for a long time to meet souls, whom I have been with in past lives and have helped me through those times. It was mentally good to embrace them again. The surges in my mind so exhilarating and yet as I awake, my memories of them seem to disappear, for during this life they have no presence.

Logically, happenings throughout the years of your life, will eventually affect the understanding of the purpose of life, so one way to go forward is to explore Sacred Cornwall's places. You visualize the absolute beauty, your feelings are so peaceful and wonderful. The sun's rays reflect on the earth, the swirling mist caress the ground and the spiritual ancient past is very evident. Opening your mind to the path of Nature, take you through to other dimensions that linger in the background of the shimmering shadows.

For somehow the earliest days, seem so different. The surface of the wondrous earth was thought to reflect the pattern and progression of the heavenly sphere. The secret energy of the Light is very sensitive to ways of Nature and was a basis for the ancient world, which is now beyond our current level of understanding.

So on entering a timeless tranquillity in Cornwall, special to you, which is close to a heavenly world, allows your mind to be open, away from the frustration of the present world. The reason for living starts to infiltrate your being, by operating in harmony with others, gives you the final purpose of life and allows you the ultimate journey along the path to eternal light.

Special Thanks to: -

The Paul Watts Cornish Picture Library for supplying the images.
Web site www.imageclick.co.uk
Eden Print for their printing and finishing.
Tor Mark for distribution of the Books

Published by: -

R & B Enterprise, Trelawney Lodge, Keveral Lane, Seaton, Cornwall PL11 3JJ
Telephone 01503 250673 Email info@imageclick.co.uk
Written by Roger Lock. Designed by Barbara Lock.
Supportive work by Barbara Davis and Viv Watts.

Roger Lock 2005   ISBN 0-9544335-2-1

Sacred Cornwall - The Heritage

First book in the series, full of facts, myths and legends, including stories of Jesus, John Wesley, King Arthur, St Michael's Ley Line, Kings Templar, The Mermaid of Zennor, Mystic Cornwall, A View from a Cornish Church, The Reason for Living and a Poem.

Sacred Cornwall - Love Stories

Second book in the series, includes stories about Thomas Hardy, Robert Stephen Hawker, Temple, The Mermaid to the Rescue, A Cornish Parent's Love Story, Kitty, The Last Day in Cornwall, Love is close yet so far away and a Poem.

Available at most Books Shops and Tourist Information Centres